Harold R. Warren

Knowing Jesus in Your Life

D0167154

Carol Anderson
with Peter Summers

MOREHOUSE PUBLISHING
Harrisburg, Pennsylvania

Copyright © Carol Anderson and Peter Summers, 1993

This edition issued by special arrangement with
Monarch Publications, Broadway House, The Broadway,
Crowborough, East Sussex TN6 1HQ England
Original Title: WHO DO YOU SAY THAT I AM?

All rights reserved.
No part of this publication may be reproduced or
transmitted in any form or by any means, electronic
or mechanical, including photocopy, recording, or any
information storage and retrieval system, without
permission in writing from the publisher.

Unless otherwise indicated, biblical quotations
are from the Revised Standard Version.

First published by Monarch, 1993
First American edition published in 1995 by

Morehouse Publishing

Editorial Office:
871 Ethan Allen Highway
Ridgefield, CT 06877

Corporate Office:
P.O. Box 1321
Harrisburg, PA 17105

Library of Congress Cataloging-in-Publication Data

Anderson, Carol, Rev.
  [Who do you say that I am?]
  Knowing Jesus in your life / Carol Anderson with Peter
Summers. — 1st American ed.
      p.   cm.
  Originally published. Who do you say that I am?
  ISBN 0-8192-1643-7
  1. Jesus Christ—Person and offices. 2. Jesus Christ—
Knowableness.   3. Christian life. I. Summers, Peter
II. Title.
BT202.A645   1995   95-3419
232—dc20   CIP

Printed in the United States of America

KNOWING JESUS IN YOUR LIFE

The Rev. Carol Anderson was one of the first women to be ordained in the Episcopal Church in the United States. She is Rector of All Saints' Parish, Beverly Hills, California, and has been recently awarded an honorary doctorate from Berkeley Divinity School at Yale.

Peter Summers has an MA in English Literature from Cambridge University, and an MFA in Film Production from UCLA Film School. He is the son of British Evangelist Don Summers. A screenwriter and filmmaker, he lives in Los Angeles.

CONTENTS

The contents of this book are the result of classes taught at All Saints' Church, Beverly Hills, California. It is the wonderful people of that parish who have taught me most about who Jesus is today.

Carol Anderson

For my mother and father, with love.

Peter Summers

ACKNOWLEDGEMENTS

I am deeply grateful for the editorial expertise of Peter Summers, Betty Kardos and Eddie Gibbs, who sacrificed both time and sanity in helping to make this book readable.

INTRODUCTION

In 1991 I had the joy of attending the enthronement of
the new Archbishop of Canterbury in Canterbury
Cathedral. The guests were required to take their seats
two hours ahead of time for security reasons. The
pageantry and processions started well before the actual
service. Members of the Royal Family, the judiciary in
their flowing robes and members of Parliament arrived.
Prelates of many churches processed, from those
arrayed in the bright finery of the Roman Catholic and
the Eastern Orthodox churches, to the simplicity of Billy
Graham in a black gown. At the end of the procession
was George Carey, the Archbishop-elect, wearing a
magnificent gold cope. Most of these people, famous in
the world or in the church, stopped as they came down
the long aisle, and acknowledged a simple cross which
rises in front of the nave. It struck me that in that place
of great beauty and splendour there was in fact only one
person of true greatness, and he was reigning from a cross.

It is the Jesus who lived, died on a cross and rose
again, the one acknowledged by so many at Canterbury
Cathedral, that I pray you will encounter in these pages,
for it has been the belief of Christians since the beginning
that knowing Jesus Christ is the most important aspect
of human life.

CHAPTER 1

'WHO DO YOU SAY THAT I AM?': LIFE'S MOST IMPORTANT QUESTION

> And Jesus went on with his disciples, to the villages of Caesarea Philippi; and on the way he asked his disciples, 'Who do people say that I am?' (Mark 8:27)

Who is Jesus? Why is he so important? A recent report in the Los Angeles Times stated that Americans as a society do not have any absolute beliefs. On the other hand, most Christians do. Believing that Jesus is central to both our lives and the whole of human history says something about those beliefs.

The focus of this book is the question Jesus asked at Caesarea Philippi: 'Who do you say that I am?' Jesus asked it of his disciples during a period of transition in his ministry, after he had spent much time in Galilee teaching about the in-breaking of the Kingdom of God, which is the restoring of a broken and hurting world to a right relationship with God. The disciples answered, 'John the Baptist; and others say, Elijah.' (Mark 8:28). He pressed them: 'But who do you say that I am?' Peter replied, 'You are the Christ,' which to them would mean the Messiah whom Israel longed for.

Many of us would not know how to answer honestly Jesus' question. Some would want to answer as Peter did, but would not really know why. Others would have legitimate questions as to what it all means. We need to look at it from several vantage points.

How we see God

There are many different views about God. The first we will consider is known as the *deist* view. Many of the founders of America were deists. They believed that God created the world and the laws governing it, and then left it alone. According to this view God is like a clockmaker who winds up a clock (the world), and lets it go, to run on its own. This is probably how most of us function except for those times when we really need God. God is not central to our day-to-day existence and does not set the direction of our lives until a time of crisis, when we seek help.

The second view is of a God who is out to spoil our fun. Often people from rigid religious backgrounds imagine a wrathful, vengeful God who cannot stand it if he sees you having fun! If you are enjoying yourself, you must be doing something wrong or immoral! People who have grown up in environments where the basic understanding of God is as a law-giver, believe that God will be angry if they are out of sync with those laws. There is no sense of a God who loves us, but of someone who waits for us to have a good time, just so he can stop it. Even people from outside of this kind of background find it difficult to relate to God, fearful that he will spoil their life.

The third view of God is that of a kind old man in the sky, a God who is the best image of somebody's grandfather. I call him the 'Hallmark card God'! He's very sweet and very loving and will never say 'No'.

There are no boundaries in life and God will always be nice.

The fourth view is one which many subscribe to: God is an amorphous, unknown force. This God is an impersonal benevolent spirit moving around the universe, a little like smog in Los Angeles! He is hard to relate to, but is referred to as 'spiritual energy'.

The Christian faith: a relationship with God

In contrast to these views is the biblical view. The God the Bible talks about is personal and involved, has qualities of personality and is engaged with his creation. The Old Testament, with its perceived images of an angry God, presents problems to many people. But the Old Testament shows God interacting with his people. He loves them, he is angry with them, he yearns for them to be faithful, he calls them to repentance, he deeply cares for them. There is a knock-down, drag-out battle between God and his people and God is always seeking to draw them back to himself, to the place of real life. Having spent most of my adult life in New York City I am convinced that God is Jewish with a little bit of Italian!

One of my favourite stories from the Old Testament is that of Abraham and Sarah. God promises the two of them a child, and that they will be the parents of many generations to come. After many years angels of God return to Abraham and repeat God's promise. (Genesis 18). Sarah overhears this conversation and starts laughing: she cannot imagine bearing a child at her age! She's passed her best years and knows this is impossible. The Lord hears her and asks why she laughs. She lies and says she didn't laugh. But Sarah becomes pregnant and the child she bears is called Isaac, the Hebrew word for 'he laughs'. (Genesis 21). God has the last laugh—and it's Isaac.

The Old Testament view of God is of a creator who speaks the world into existence and interacts with it constantly. God cajoles, loves, judges, walks with and finally delivers his people. He is above all a God who is active in his creation, a God whose purpose is for us to be in fellowship with him. He deeply desires a relationship with us. The Judaeo–Christian faith is not about principles, and it's not about 'religion'. It's about relationship. Somewhere deep inside all of us is the desire for a lasting and deep relationship with God, something that sets our hearts on a steady course through life.

God's deepest desire for us is a 'peace which passes all understanding,' a sense of security which continues no matter what happens in life, a joy which cannot be broken. Pascal, the French philosopher, said that each of us has a God-shaped void that we try to fill with things that never satisfy. Only God can fill it. Saint Augustine said, 'Our hearts are restless until they rest in God'.

Three ways of coming to faith

The New Testament reveals at least three ways in which people became followers of Jesus. Saint Paul had a dramatic conversion on the road to Damascus, a powerful encounter with Jesus and a profound change of life. If you've ever watched much Christian television you may think that this is the only way one ever becomes a Christian. I have seen it happen often. I gave a hard-driving real estate agent a book to read on the Christian faith. It took him a long time to finish it, but when he had, he came back to my office, slammed the book down on my desk and said, 'I believe it'. He gave the basics of the faith back to me in his own words; he had understood it, and his whole life changed overnight. Most of us would like that to happen, but that is only one way. The apostle John shows us a second way. In the New Testament John was always there with Jesus, at his side, quietly following him. Jesus called him the 'beloved disciple'. Like him, some of us have always believed, from as far back as we can remember. From the time we were children, we have been followers of Jesus. There are people who agonize over faith, asking question after question, and that makes some of us whose faith is sure think there is something wrong with us. Why aren't we struggling? Some of us just seem to have always known God and believed in Jesus.

A lot of us are like Peter, our third example. Peter followed Jesus, but he had endless questions and struggles. He was like someone who goes to church on Sunday, listens to the sermon, is moved by the worship, finds it all makes sense, then it falls apart on Monday. Peter would take two steps forward and one step back. He was the first to publicly declare Jesus as the Messiah and then a short time later, when Jesus was arrested, he denied ever knowing him. I am a Peter. If I hadn't been a Peter and struggled through many hills and valleys in coming to the Christian faith, I would never be where I am today.

It is important to remember that God does not despise our questions. All of us come to faith in a different way. Some of us are like Saint Paul, and it all arrives in a blinding flash. Many people would like it to be that way, but most often it is not. People who have a personality like mine wouldn't trust a major emotional cataclysm like that. It would not be 'me'.

What brings people to faith? The Scriptures show that it is God at work in each of us drawing us back to himself. Whether we acknowledge him or not, God is at work seeking to reconcile us to himself. Many of us can see this only in retrospect; looking back, we see how God has been at work in our lives all along. I would like to share with you certain key moments in my own life, times when I came to rethink my own faith, and when I discovered a God unlike any I'd ever imagined.

I come from a very small town in New Jersey, from a moderately conservative family. Less than three months after I started college I became involved in a civil rights demonstration, and I was arrested. The demonstration was the most exciting thing that had ever happened to me. I became part of the 1960's political and social turmoil. My fellow activists and I believed that by protest and action we could create a better society and actually change the world. I was so swept up in that belief that during my college years I was arrested several times. It became more important to me than my studies.

As part of that commitment I spent a brief part of my senior year as one of the few white people at a black college in South Carolina. It was a very powerful experience for me as I saw appalling poverty at close hand for the first time, and the gap between my fellow students' lives and my own. I realized the magnitude of the change needed in America. I was reading idealistic social philosophy, but I realized that something radical would have to change for the world to be put right.

One day I was out walking with a roommate, a young black lady from one of the islands off the South Carolina coast. She was frightened because the state was one of the most conservative and it wasn't good for a black person to be seen walking with a white. She was very jumpy. Before long a pick-up truck, which had followed me around a lot while I was there, pulled up beside us. I looked around and realized that the men in the truck were members of a white racist organization I had heard about. My friend said, 'Just get out of here, this is trouble,' and fled. Innocent as I was, I thought people could just be reasoned with, so I stayed and waited. A man jumped out of the truck carrying a baseball bat. He stared at me and called me 'Nigger-lover'. Then he lifted the baseball bat and struck my knees. I fell to the ground and another man started kicking me. A car mercifully came by and the men left before any further damage could be done.

My knees were badly hurt (even now I can't kneel for long in church) but more importantly, my life changed that day. I saw in the eyes of those men a hatred so deep, an evil so powerful that it was more than just human: it was a larger evil, a violence that could take over a group of people. I looked into the face of the leader while they were assaulting me and kept asking, 'Why are you doing this?' All he could say was, 'You nigger-lover,' over and over again. There was such bitterness and hatred inside of him. I realized that for all the idealism I and many others were espousing, there was a fundamental need to change the human heart before any real progress could be made. What I saw in that man's face was the fact that behind so much of the disorder of the world are some very broken people who, when banded together, become a very effective force for evil. And I began to question whether social protest and changing laws alone could solve the problem.

Later in my life, when I graduated from seminary, in 1970, I could not, as a woman, be ordained in the Episcopal Church. Hoping this would change, I spent a year as a chaplain intern at Massachusetts General Hospital in Boston. I was assigned to the cardiac and paediatric intensive care units. I saw most of the pre-operative heart patients and the families of a lot of children who were seriously ill.

Open-heart surgery was not the fairly routine event it is today and the outcome was not as certain. As part of my work I would visit patients and pray with them before surgery. I had a two-point prayer. The first point dealt with the fear of letting go and losing control, giving way to the doctor's anesthesia, and the second asked God to take care of the families who waited. The prayer was sensitive and seemed to help, but I felt like a fraud, because I didn't really know very well the God to whom I was praying or whether or not he would respond. This feeling of being a fake went on for some time with growing discomfort on my part.

One day I went to see Harold, a New England farmer who was scheduled for bypass surgery. He asked me if I would pray for him the next day before his operation. That morning I went to the hospital with great reluctance. I wasn't looking forward to it, and took my time getting to see the man. I talked to nurses, other patients, anyone so that I would avoid praying for Harold. I climbed the stairs (all eleven flights) to his floor, confident that if I stalled he would already be on his way to surgery! I even planned the apologies I would make to him later. But he was there, waiting for me with a smile on his face.

'I knew you'd come,' he told me, and I said I wouldn't have missed it for anything! He had been prepared for surgery, hooked up to IVs, and he was waiting to be wheeled out, so I only had a few minutes. I sat down, took his hand and started my usual two-point prayer. I hadn't said more than four or five words before I had an incredible feeling of power flowing through my body. I lost all sense of what I was saying. The words were no longer mine. It was a different prayer. I was aware enough to know that something else was happening, but I had no idea what it was. Harold kept pulling my arm, keeping a tight grip on me. When the prayer was finished I was thoroughly disoriented. Harold simply said, 'I'm alright now.' I staggered out into the hallway and leaned against the wall, drained and exhausted. I returned to the chaplain's office and slept for some time.

When I woke I put it all out of my mind and started my afternoon rounds. Later, when I tried to see Harold, I couldn't find him. He wasn't in the intensive care unit or in the recovery room and, thankfully, not in the morgue. Then a nurse told me that Harold's doctor wanted to see me. I hurried nervously to his office, sure there would be trouble waiting for me when I arrived. I was 25, with the fear level of a 9-year-old!

'What did you do to Harold?' he asked.

'I don't know. What's happened to him? I can't find him,' I replied.

'We came to take him to surgery and he said, "I'm not going, I'm alright now. I want another catherization before you do anything. There's nothing the matter with me."'

The doctor pointed to two sets of X-rays on his wall. The first was taken the previous day, clearly showing massive arterial blockage. The second set, taken that morning, showed the arteries now open and unblocked.

'Every time I questioned Harold he said, "The chaplain did it!" What did you do?'

I couldn't answer him because I didn't know. I knew something had taken place, but I couldn't explain it. And it took me six years before I could even begin to tell that story because I had no frame of reference for a God who would, in fact, heal anybody. I had no theology for dealing with this, no understanding of it whatsoever.

This kind of thing never happened again while I was at the hospital, and I just blocked it out as if it had happened to somebody else. That was a second transitional moment for me because I, like a lot of others, thought of God as a force who moved around and through people, but never connected with them in a personal, transforming way.

For a short time I went to New York City and worked for the Episcopal Mission Society. From there I went to St James' Church in Manhattan, on the Upper East Side, a very well-to-do place, with many wealthy business leaders as members. I spent seven and a half very happy years at St James', but at the same time a lot of the pain of the world began to sink in. The death of people, especially children, the emotional pain and toll of life, marriages collapsing, all began to weigh heavily on me.

I'd been trained to listen, rather like a therapist. I had a sympathetic ear, but I'd been told that all I could do about people's pain was to listen and 'be there'. I was trained in the Rogerian method, client-centred therapy, so if someone said to me 'I've just killed my husband!', I was supposed to reply, flatly, 'you've just killed your husband.' My responses were not allowed to impose any of my own views or values, just confirm that I was listening.

One day a woman came to me sobbing, telling me that her husband had been beating her. The first words out of my mouth were, 'That really sucks!' While I was trying to make sense of what I'd just said, she looked at me and replied, 'You understand!' The force of her response made me aware that I had to become personally involved if I were to help. At the same time, I knew that I could never change her life for her; I needed to know if lives like hers could be redeemed, could have meaning restored to them. I finally had to ask myself if there might be more to God than I'd thought all along. Could God directly change this woman?

Gradually, these questions began to nag away at me: the problem of evil, what to do with a world that is broken and sick, and how human lives can be changed. I read a lot of the great literature, hoping to find ideas or a philosophy which could change lives. At the end of my time at the parish I began to wonder if there wasn't more to the Christian faith than I had thought. Could God make a bigger difference? One of the associates on our staff used to badger me with questions. 'You don't know who Jesus is,' he'd say, 'you're a pagan!' I'd answer back, 'You're a fundamentalist!', which was the worst thing I could think of to call him! Our friendly arguments were very challenging.

During this period, I began reading the New Testament anew, with lots of questions in my head and heart, and there I encountered the person of Jesus. I saw that he was confronting evil, healing people who were sick and broken, and he was talking about the Kingdom of God and 'new life'. Thus began the journey which culminated in my becoming a convinced disciple of Jesus Christ. God became alive to me and was working in my life, and he was able to change the lives of other people as well.

CHAPTER 2

WHO IS JESUS?

Christians believe in a God who acts, not one who is remote. The God of the Scriptures is involved with our lives. He interacts with his creation. He is a God who loves, cajoles and gets angry with us. He cares so much that he sent us his Son. The most important question we can ask in our lives is 'Who is Jesus Christ?'. If we are to answer that question we must examine the evidence. So many people reject Jesus on the basis of inadequate information. There is an objectivity to the Christian faith that our generation tends to ignore.

An historian's view

Let us first look at the person of Jesus, not from a believer's viewpoint but from that of an objective historian. Michael Grant, an historian formerly at Cambridge University in England, wrote a book called *Jesus, An Historian's Review of the Gospels* (Macmillan, 1992). It is an excellent book. Grant does not write as a Christian: he analyses the four Gospels (Matthew, Mark, Luke and John) and considers the portrait of Jesus offered there. He emphasizes that it is important to understand that the accounts written in the Gospels are not like newspaper stories. They are not consecutive narratives or a daily digest of Jesus' ministry. They are accounts written by different people, seeing the same situation, and recording it from their own perspectives. They are committed not simply to telling stories, but to making sure that the point of each narrative is communicated.

If several people were to see a traffic accident, it is certain that each person witnessing it would describe the accident in their own particular way. We each have our own way of seeing things. Some people see life in a much more colourful way than others; some see the broad sweep, others the details. The Gospel writers were like that; they had individual ways of writing about Jesus.

Michael Grant looked at the gospel texts and commented that although this is not the way one writes history, the material is historical, the stories have the ring of authenticity. For example, there are many embarrassing stories left in the text. Some of the disciples are not pictured very positively. Peter, who became the first Bishop of the Church, sometimes comes across unfavourably—one day he was committed to Jesus and the next he denied knowing him. It makes no sense to write a book about such a man and make him out to be a fool.

Not only are awkward stories retained, but inconsistencies as well. The resurrection stories are described in different ways; different people were there. Although some people try to make them all harmonize, Grant sees authenticity in the inconsistency. The Bible doesn't answer every question we have.

Michael Grant says the writings in the Gospels show the desire to tell the truth, warts and all. It is useful for comparison to look at some of the documents that didn't make it into the New Testament. There are a number of apocryphal books which are not an accepted part of the canon of Scripture and which the early Church rejected. Stories are put together by people claiming that Jesus walked through walls, flew through the air, and turned lumps of clay into birds. When the Bible was pieced together, these stories were rejected; they lacked what Grant refers to as the 'ring' of authenticity.

The followers of Jesus were very careful to try to preserve the memory of all the things he said and did, because they wanted to be able to repeat it. At that time, storytelling was at the heart of memory and communication. Stories were learned, treasured, told and retold in a much more vigorous way than they are today. This, too, leads us to believe that authenticity is at the heart of the Gospel stories.

The objective facts about Jesus

What are the objective facts about Jesus? What is the basic information? He was born in Bethlehem, and grew up in Nazareth, neither place a centre of influence. His family was probably middle-class. He learned the carpentry trade from his father. He was trained in Jewish life and law in the synagogue, the centre of the community. Very early in life, he was drawn to religious questions. Luke 2:41ff says that when Jesus was 12 he stayed behind in Jerusalem after the Passover. His parents didn't realize it, thinking he was in the company of friends. They returned and searched for him for three days and found him in the temple listening to the teachers and asking them questions, and all who heard him were amazed at his understanding and his answers. So, as a young man, Jesus was already thinking about religious questions and was regarded as having insight by the rabbis.

Nothing is known about Jesus from the age of twelve until about thirty. If you look in the New Age bookstores you will find a whole host of volumes purporting to tell you the truth about Jesus' lost years. Some suggest he went to India and became a guru, others say he went to England or Japan. Yet the cultural and religious reality of Jesus' day suggests otherwise. He probably lived with his parents, practised carpentry and spent time at the synagogue. It is almost certain that he never left Palestine, apart from the period as a baby when his parents fled to Egypt with him to avoid Herod's murderous intentions: no reputable scholar will tell you any differently.

The early stories about his life related in the Bible probably came from Mary, his mother. Mary was one of the group of people who followed Jesus when he began his public ministry. Scholars have suggested that one of the ways in which the New Testament was compiled was as the disciples, Mary and some of the brothers of Jesus, sat down after the resurrection and ascension, when Jesus was no longer with them, and told stories. The disciples would ask what Jesus had been like as a child. Mary would talk about her sense that God had a special mission for her son. Only with hindsight had these become apparent: 'Mary (had) kept all these things, pondering them in her heart'. (Luke 2:19).

Jesus began his public ministry at the age of thirty when he was baptized. John the Baptist was the leader of a reform movement within Judaism. Jesus asked John to baptize him into the repentance, or new life, that he was preaching. When Jesus came up out of the water, we are told, the clouds opened and God's voice came from heaven saying, 'You are my beloved son; with you I am well pleased' (Mark 1:11). It was a time of 'anointing', or call to ministry. This is a relatively common biblical occurrence. It happened in the Old Testament: Moses was called, so were Abraham and Sarah, and so was David. They were all called in special ways and emerged from private life into public ministry. And this is what happened to Jesus.

In the tradition of the Old Testament, the 'voice from heaven' is bestowing God's authority onto Jesus.

In Old Testament times, the father would lay hands on the eldest son and bestow all the assets and traditions of the family onto him—not just the family name but the family leadership, the authority—the family's sense of identity.

When a bishop in the catholic tradition administers the sacrament of confirmation, he or she lays hands on the individual and asks the Holy Spirit to fill them with new life. In confirmation, the bishop is saying, 'All that God wants for your life I am conferring on you and giving to you.'

God's anointing of Jesus gave him the authority to announce the coming of the Kingdom of God. This is the essence of Jesus' public ministry. He talked about the in-breaking, through his life and ministry, of the things of God that were lost at the Fall (we shall discuss this later).

Jesus gathered twelve people around him, ostensibly to carry on his teachings, and then at the end of three years he was condemned for what was, within the Jewish community, blasphemy (and possibly, in the eyes of the Roman authorities, treason). He was put to death by crucifixion—a painful and agonizing execution. Three days later he was claimed by his followers to be alive. That is the story in objective outline.

Jesus' own claims for himself

As we look beyond the objective outline, we begin to realize that Jesus expressed some radical ideas about himself in the things he said and did. Let's consider the claims Jesus made for himself.

One with God

Jesus claimed to be one with God—not merely a part of God but one with him (John 10:30). The Nicene Creed says of Jesus that he was 'begotten, not made, being of one substance with the Father.' A lot of New Age teaching says that we are all a part of God. The New Testament does not teach that. We are not all God. We may have attributes of God, qualities of God, but are not made of the same substance. Yet Jesus is boldly described as being the same as God. If you had been a faithful Jew in Jesus' time you would have shrunk away from even saying the name of God, yet Jesus claimed that 'I and the Father are one', which was a startling proclamation. He claimed a unique relationship with God which no *faithful* person would proclaim. When the Pharisees, the religious authorities, heard such statements they would put their fingers in their ears.

Startling claims

The Gospel of John records many of the claims of Jesus. 'I am the light of the world' (8:12); 'I am the bread of life' (6:35); 'I am the way, and the truth and the life; no one comes to the Father, but by me' (14:6). These statements are quite exclusive. Jesus talks about himself being the way to God. He talked about coming to bestow life: 'I came that they may have life and have it abundantly' (10:10). Jesus is making claims for himself which are startling if he is just another religious teacher, another 'good man'.

Jesus claimed that he fulfilled Old Testament prophecy about the Messiah (Luke 4:21). He talked about himself as the central focus of love and commitment (John 3:36). When Caiaphas, the high priest, asked 'Are you the Christ, the son of the Blessed?', he answered, 'I am' (Mark 14:61–62).

In the most astonishing claim of all, Jesus claims that he can forgive sins. Nobody within the Jewish community would ever claim to forgive sins; only God could do that. Yet Jesus claimed and did so (Matthew 9:6; Mark 2:5–7).

Jesus boldly presented himself as the direct authority for his teachings. The scribes and the Pharisees would not do this. They would never make straightforward pronouncements, but always quoted Scripture or a well-known rabbi as their authority on a point. On the other hand Jesus would say, 'You have heard that it was said . . . but I say to you' (Matthew 5:21; 5:27). He ascribed to himself great authority. It was as if God himself was speaking through Jesus. Today we are very used to hearing self-proclaimed experts offer themselves as authorities on practically everything. In Jesus' time a pious Jew would never offer his own opinions as if they were definitive.

Jesus spoke of himself as the judge of the world at the end of history. 'Before him will be gathered all the nations, and he will separate them one from another as a shepherd separates the sheep from the goats' (Matthew 25:32). In Jewish belief God alone was judge.

Jesus again seems to put himself in the same place as God.

Spoken of in the Old Testament

> For to us a child is born, to us a son is given; and the government will be upon his shoulder, and his name will be called 'Wonderful Counsellor, Mighty God, Everlasting Father, Prince of Peace.' (Isaiah 9:6).

These words are often repeated at Christmas services. This is part of the prophecy, or 'forth-telling', of Isaiah, a prophet of the Old Testament. There are a number of opinions as to who this was written about. Some suggest it was about a longed-for mighty ruler who would release Israel from its oppression. Yet at the very heart of Israel's longings, then and even now, was a desire for the Messiah to come. Prayers were said in the temple for the coming of the Messiah. More than a mighty ruler, he was seen as a king who would release Israel from the oppressions of enemies. This particular prophecy Jesus took and used to describe himself.

Isaiah's prophecies go on: 'There shall come forth a shoot from the stump of Jesse, and a branch shall grow out of his roots.' (Isaiah 11:1). 'From the stump of Jesse,' really means out of the lineage of Jesse. The first chapter of Matthew, verse 6, provides a genealogy of Jesus, showing his coming forth from Jesse (the gospel of Matthew was specifically written to speak to the Jews, and it was important to show Jesus fulfilling this prophecy).

> He was despised and rejected by men; a man of sorrows, and acquainted with grief; and as one from whom men hid their faces he was despised, and we esteemed him not.

Surely he has borne our griefs and carried our sorrows; yet we esteemed him stricken, smitten by God, and afflicted. But he was wounded for our transgressions, he was bruised for our iniquities; upon him was the chastisement that made us whole, and with his stripes (the marks of being beaten) we are healed. All we like sheep have gone astray; we have turned every one to his own way; and the Lord has laid on him the iniquity of us all (Isaiah 53:3–6).

This is the portrait of the Man of Sorrows, one of the most powerful chapters in all of the Bible. It is about a particular person and what was going to happen to him. Many of the particulars in this prophecy were fulfilled in the life of Jesus.

The Spirit of the Lord God is upon me, because the Lord has anointed me to bring good tidings to the afflicted; he has sent me to bind up the brokenhearted, to proclaim liberty to the captives, and the opening of the prison to those who are bound. (Isaiah 61:1).

The Gospel of Luke records Jesus reading this passage in a synagogue in Nazareth and announcing, 'Today this scripture has been fulfilled in your hearing' (Luke 4:21). It seems that Jesus saw himself as the fulfilment of the hopes of Israel, as the Messiah, and described himself in that way. He saw his ministry, except for the military and political aspects of it which he rejected, as that which was hoped for in the Old Testament.

But you, O Bethlehem Ephrathah, who are little to be among the clans of Judah, from you shall come forth to me one who is to be ruler in Israel, whose origin is from old, from ancient days. (Micah 5:2).

The prophet Micah foretold a ruler from Bethlehem, the place of Jesus' birth.

> Rejoice greatly, O daughter of Zion! Shout aloud, O daughter of Jerusalem! Lo, your king comes to you; triumphant and victorious is he, humble and riding on an ass, on a colt the foal of an ass (Zechariah 9:9).

Zechariah's prophecy pictures the Messiah entering Jerusalem on a colt, which is what Jesus actually did (see Matthew 21:1–11). Jesus fulfilled so many of the prophetic texts of the Old Testament.

The disciples were prepared to die for Jesus

Jesus said a lot about himself directly and indirectly. But the last and most important element in the New Testament which supports the claims of Jesus as Messiah is his disciples. The Gospels tell us that the group of followers Jesus called to be his disciples were not the choicest people available. To put it politely, anybody in their right mind would not have chosen them! He chose zealots, radicals, and people who couldn't look after money. They were immature, dysfunctional rabble-rousers and hot-heads.

There is a wonderful memo that begins: 'To Jesus Christ from the Jerusalem Personnel Agency. We have interviewed all your candidates for disciples and we find that they are all people who will not serve your company well.' It took apart each one of the disciples and concluded, 'However, the only one we have found who might actually be of use to you is Judas!' Jesus surrounded himself with imperfect disciples, people just like us.

The disciples were continually hoping that Jesus would fulfil their own agendas. They kept asking why he didn't display his divine power, overthrow the Romans and sort everything out. Jesus responded that this was not the way God's Kingdom would come into being.

On one occasion, the disciples were talking about which one of them would be the greatest in the Kingdom, who Jesus really favoured the most (see Luke 9:46–48). Jesus questioned them about their discussions and told them that if they were to be followers of his, they must become like little children.

At the last supper, when Jesus washed the feet of his disciples, he showed them that the style of his kingdom is not about powerbases, but about service (John 13:5–15).

Judas may have betrayed Jesus because he hadn't lived up to the political expectations of the Messiah and wanted to force his hand. He hoped that Jesus would reveal himself to be a great military leader. But Jesus didn't respond that way.

Immediately after he was arrested the disciples deserted him. For three years he had talked to them about what God was doing in the world, and showed them how to go about ministering in God's way; now that he was arrested they were just plain scared. Yet after the resurrection this desperate group of faithless disciples became the greatest testimony to the reality of Jesus. Although all of them fled at his arrest, within days they were transformed into people who, almost without exception, would eventually die for their faith in Jesus.

How many of us would die for somebody who was not who he said he was? How many of us would give our lives for somebody who was just a great religious teacher? How many of us would give our lives for somebody who said he was God and yet was crucified? The disciples changed radically and bore powerful witness to Jesus' life and resurrection. So I add to all the objective truths about Jesus, and to all the claims he made for himself, the testimony of the disciples after the resurrection. They believed that Jesus was uniquely the Son of God and the Messiah. Look at the change in the lives of the people who lived closest to Jesus and his teaching. They began to act and sound like him.

One of my favourite stories in the New Testament is from the book of Acts. The first time that Peter and John return to the temple to worship after their ministry begins they meet a man who is crippled. He had spent his whole life begging at the temple door. He wanted money from them, but they had no money to give. Peter said, 'I have no silver and gold, but I give you what I have; in the name of Jesus Christ of Nazareth, walk.' (Acts 3:6). The man jumped up, and the Bible describes him leaping and dancing and praising God. Peter and John had taken on the ministry of Jesus, doing what he did.

Many centuries ago, so the story goes, Thomas Aquinas, one of Christendom's greatest theologians, visited Pope Urban IV in Rome. He walked into the Pope's chamber and was confronted by a huge wooden desk, laden with silver and gold. Urban IV and his stewards were going through the coins. The Pope turned to Thomas and said 'No more does the Church have to say, "silver and gold have I none."' Thomas looked at him, sighed, and said 'True, Holy Father, but neither can she now say "In the name of Jesus of Nazareth get up and walk."' Jesus came to bring new life and healing, to recreate God's life in us.

What does this mean for us?

This is a book about getting to know the essential Jesus. Not a mystical or fanciful Jesus, but the Jesus who lived like us and called disciples, people who acted just like we do, to follow him. Just as he went around the countryside and called each of his disciples by name, so now Jesus calls us by name, touching our lives and creating a longing for his presence in our hearts. He has drawn you to read this book and he is asking you to consider his claims, to ask yourself if he is worth following.

C. S. Lewis, a professor of literature at Oxford and Cambridge, had been challenged by somebody who said that Jesus was just a great religious teacher and a great man. Lewis responded by saying that anybody who says the things Jesus said about himself, and accepts from other people the claim that he is the Messiah would either be a lunatic (on the level with someone who calls himself a poached egg), or he is who he says he is, and is the Son of God. (*Mere Christianity*, p. 56, Macmillan, 1960). Jesus is too human, too sane, too well-balanced, too well-put-together to be a lunatic. The balance of his personality shows him not to be delusional by nature. Therefore, he must be who he says he is. Lewis concludes that you must either call him the devil himself or the Lord of all history.

We cannot make Jesus in our own image. We have to let him speak for himself, and then accept or reject him on the basis of who he says he is and who other people close to him say he is. Keep asking questions of him. Once you have made up your mind that he is who he claims to be, he will make a claim on your life and your life will not be the same. It will change your life.

To be a follower of Jesus is a radical step. It is not to be religious: it is to have a relationship with a person who, in fact, calls into question everything about our lives and who turns us around and moves us in directions that go against all that the world thinks is important.

CHAPTER 3

GOD'S ORIGINAL INTENTION FOR US

> . . . then the Lord God formed man of dust from the ground, and breathed into his nostrils the breath of life; and man became a living being. (Genesis 2:7).

If you read through the first two chapters of Genesis (the first book in the Bible), you will find that God's original intention for humankind was extraordinary. We were created in God's image, which means that we have within us unique attributes of God—for example, love, nurturing and will. A closeness to God was intended, as well. Humans were to be able to walk closely with God, to know him and themselves well.

There has been a lot of battling about the meaning and purpose of this book. The best scholars believe that Genesis was never intended to be either a book of history or of science. It does not contradict science necessarily, but it wasn't designed to be a scientific textbook: it was meant to be a book of description, communicating how certain things came to be in our universe. We must be careful about the questions we ask of the book of Genesis, or of any other book in the Bible.

The first part of the book of Genesis is a writer's attempt to explain, under the guidance of God's spirit, how our world started and what God's intention was at the beginning. God wanted a perfect and proper relationship with his creation.

'Adam' is the Hebrew word for 'man', and 'Eve' means 'woman'. The intention of creating humankind was that there would be, on the earth, a creature who had a great deal of God's personality and life. It's a wonderful story, God breathing life into the dust (Genesis 2:7). You can read it literally or as poetry. Either way, feel the force of the language. The Hebrew word for breathing life is *ruach*. Hebrew is such a descriptive language; often the sound of the word describes its meaning. The passage is talking about God taking something very basic and very simple out of creation and breathing his life into it. This is not to say that humans became God, but that we took on the breath of God, the Spirit of God, the life of God in us, so that we became intimately related to God's life. If you have ever had a child you know that the child is flesh of your own flesh, bone of your own bone and breath of your own breath. There is life that you put into a child, that makes all the difference in the world. You know them as your own flesh, and you cherish their creation.

In the beginning of Genesis we find that God intended us to be of his own essence, his own life, his own Spirit. Humans were created in God's likeness—not in the sense of looking like God in a physical or even spiritual sense, but in the sense of having his attributes such as love and hope.

God also gave humankind dominion over creation. The word 'dominion' means 'stewardship', to care for the world as a parent would care for a child. Just as good parents do not abuse their children, so dominion does not mean to subdue or to plunder; it means having a loving relationship with the universe and the environment. Much of our relationship to the environment today would be improved if we took Genesis seriously.

God made only one stipulation to the first humans: 'You may freely eat of every tree of the garden; but of the tree of knowledge of good and evil you shall not eat, for in the day that you eat of it you shall die'. (Genesis 2:16). Man and woman would exercise authority over everything they had been given, within limits. What does this mean? Remember this is a story we are telling: the tree was a symbol that humankind would not have authority over God. We would not have that omniscience that God has, but would be subject to him. God is the Creator, we are the created. He is God and we are not. Those were the terms of the relationship. Much of New Age religion proclaims that we are God. That is not biblical faith.

What went wrong?

It is interesting that there is no notion in the Creation story about where the serpent came from. The serpent just appears as a tempter and speaks: 'Did God say, "You shall not eat of any tree of the garden?"' (Genesis 3:1). When the tempter whispered in Eve's ear, he was saying, 'Why are you letting God lord it over you? Why are you letting some other one tell you what to do? You should be able to make up your own mind about your own life.' We want to be our own god; we like to do what we want, when we want to, and heaven help them if someone tells us otherwise.

Independence

When I was nine years old my mother told me not to climb a particular tree in our large back yard. I hadn't really noticed the tree before this directive, but it was as if runway lights appeared from nowhere and drew me instantly towards it! I climbed into it and promptly fell out and broke both my wrists. My wrists hurt badly, but what would have hurt worse was my mother finding out that I had done something I wasn't supposed to. So you know what I did? This is an indication of how wilful I was: I fashioned popsicle (lolly) sticks into splints and wrapped them around my wrists with dish towels. And I stayed away from my mother as much as I could, until my wrists healed. It wasn't until I was in college and carrying heavy books that one of the bones popped out and a doctor, taking one look at them, in horror asked me, 'Who set your wrists?' I had been so caught up in my own rebellion in climbing that tree that I could not admit that I'd done anything wrong.

We like our independence and do not like to be under authority. Many people move on to another church or another religion if they don't like what God seems to be saying in their present one. They will even go so far as to 'change the rules' to accord with what they want. The serpent was telling Eve to think for herself. Who wants to be under the authority of anybody, let alone God? When you're grown up you think you've left all that behind. 'Be free,' the serpent was saying. So God's judgment was set aside.

Blame and shame

So when the woman saw that the tree was good for food, and that it was a delight to the eyes, and that the tree was to be desired to make one wise, she took of its fruit and ate; and she also gave some to her husband, and he ate. Then the eyes of both were opened, and they knew that they were naked; . . .' (Genesis 3:6–7).

That's what I call learning by experience! But something happened inside Adam and Eve when this took place, and not what they expected. The original relationship with God was lost. There was a sense of being tainted. If you've ever done anything that you regret deeply, you know that it follows you all through your life. There is a feeling that something in you has shifted and you don't like yourself very much. You carry it around and can't really wipe it away. God had said that if Adam and Eve ate the 'forbidden fruit' they would die, they would lose their close relationship with God. It was so.

Eve gave the fruit to Adam and he blamed her for his disobedience. Now a lot of the put-down of women throughout history has come from this particular passage. There was a wonderful cartoon in the New Yorker magazine which had God pointing to Adam, Adam to Eve, and Eve to the serpent. Everyone is trying to shift the blame; no one wants to take responsibility for what goes on in their own lives.

I read an article in a magazine about the court system in New York. It related that in nearly all court cases brought before a judge the defence held to the position that it wasn't the defendant's fault. It was the defendant's background, environment, diet or something else. Instead of just saying 'There is something in me that makes me do wrong,' and accepting responsibility, we human beings want to blame others.

There is a disposition in us which makes us want our own way. In the story of Adam and Eve, the Bible doesn't tell us where this comes from, it just tells us that it's there, and is evident by the choices that we make. Now what happens with this 'freedom', this movement into a wonderful land where God no longer has any authority over us? What happened to Adam and Eve and what happens to us when we seek control of our own lives? Look at Genesis 3 verse 7 again: 'Then the eyes of both were opened, and they knew that they were naked . . .'. That's the first thing that happened: shame. They were afraid of letting anyone see who they were. This had nothing to do with wearing clothes or not wearing clothes. Here were people who had been totally open to each other and to God, people with nothing to hide. Now they realized that they were naked, that their brokenness showed, and they wanted to be able to cover themselves. The very showing of themselves made them afraid. Have you ever felt that way yourself when you know you've done something wrong? If you've hurt somebody or really upset a relationship. You can't look that person in the eye, can you? That's what happened to Adam and Eve when they disobeyed God.

Hiding from God

> And they heard the sound of the Lord God walking in the garden in the cool of the day, and the man and his wife hid themselves from the presence of the Lord God among the trees of the garden. (Genesis 3:8).

The second thing their so-called freedom made them do was to hide from God. How does that happen for us today? How do we hide from God? Drugs, alcohol, sex, keeping busy, even religion—all these are ways of running away. The underlying assumption behind all this running is that God is after us in a way that is bad. When we are estranged from God, we think of him as someone who will spoil our lives. Adam and Eve ran and hid from the one who loved them enough to create them.

'But the Lord God called to the man, and said to him, "Where are you?"' (Genesis 3:9). That is an incredibly pregnant and poignant phrase. 'Where are you?' It's not just, 'Where are you hiding?', but, 'What has become of you, what have you got yourself into?' It's an existential question. 'With all this freedom, what has happened to you? Are you really free?' Adam had become fearful of God. God was now seen as the enemy—one who judged and one to be feared, not as one who loved. It was the dawn of the fear of God.

We think that if God finds out what we've done he is going to be really angry at us. We long for God, but in the name of our own freedom, we run from him. Instead of being free we find ourselves shameful, hiding, fearful and blaming others. There is something within us that longs to be close to God, but for the sake of our independence, we run.

Spiritual death

The fruit of our disobedience to God is spiritual death: God's light in us grows dimmer and dimmer. That is what death really means: the life God intended for us, in union with him, is lost. When someone physically dies, their breath passes out of their body. Sometimes it's peaceful, sometimes it isn't, but you can see the whole passage from life to death. In-spiration, the Spirit coming in, becomes ex-piration, the Spirit leaving. What we learn in Genesis is that when we choose to separate ourselves from God, spiritual death begins. His breath of life in us becomes shallow.

I was talking to a very successful young man who was struggling over whether or not he was going to become a Christian. He said that the one time he realized the need for a Saviour was that time during the day when he wasn't busy working, when his girlfriend wasn't around, when there was nothing on the television, nothing to read, nothing to eat, nothing to do, when he was left by himself. Then he realized just how profoundly lonely he was. That is the closest thing I know of to spiritual death. He was left with only himself. On his resume, he would look wonderful to anyone. He was successful, he made a lot of money, and ninety-nine per cent of the time he felt happy. But it was that one per cent of the time, when he was left by himself and had nothing to keep him from looking at himself, that he realized that at the heart of him was 'death'. Loneliness puts us in touch with that sense of death. Outside of a relationship with God we are left with spiritual death. We do not know in our hearts that we are loved and accepted and that somebody in this universe rejoices in the fact that we are alive.

Where does this leave us?

I think this alienation from God that the Bible calls sin leaves us broken-hearted, sad, and dying. A part of us never feels adequate about who we are. There is a tremendous fear inside us that if we really show ourselves to others, they will not like us. It is as if there is a pool of sadness inside each one of us. When I stand in the pulpit on a Sunday morning and look out over the congregation, and am telling a story that really touches somebody's life, there is often an extraordinary number of people weeping. When God's love is talked about, the pool of sadness which has filled up over the years with all of the sorrow, hurt and longing of their lives overflows and they cry.

In my first parish in New York when I was newly ordained, I received a phone call from a well-known secular psychiatrist. He said that someone had told him about me at a cocktail party, and suggested that I would make a good counsellor for one of his patients who he believed had a spiritual problem. He asked me to see the patient who had been in therapy with him for twelve years. 'I've come to believe that this person's problem is really spiritual and not psychological,' he said. The man came by to see me and after twelve years of psychotherapy he knew every nuance of his personality. He knew everything about himself: what was wrong with his father, what was wrong with his mother, what was going wrong with his marriage, what was happening at work—everything. I sat and listened and didn't know what to say to him.

'After all the time of getting to know myself,' he went on, 'I still don't like myself.' I thought for a moment and said, 'Instead of blaming everyone in your life for what has happened to you, have you ever confessed the things that you've done wrong and asked for God's forgiveness?'

'No, I've just come to understand them, I've never confessed them,' he replied.

I put on my stole, gave him a prayer book, and told him that he needed to admit to God and to me what he had done in his life—not just what had been done to him, but what he had done. I wanted him to name it all. I told him we could take as long as he needed, just to go through everything, item by item. And he went through the whole thing. Twelve years of psychotherapy meant that a whole load of garbage came out, and with his permission I share that with you. Every once in a while he would say to me, 'But I did this because . . .'

'Don't bother to tell me why you did it, just tell me what you've done, tell God what you've done', I would reply.

When he started his hands were rigid, his face was tight, and his body was ramrod straight. He was desperate when he came to see me because he could not break loose from whatever was going on inside of him. The more he talked, the more he began to relax. His body began to loosen up and in the middle of the whole thing he began to cry. Then he started to sob and said, over and over again, 'I'm so sorry. I'm so sorry. I'm so sorry.'

He continued: 'I feel like all those tears inside of me are cleansing tears. They're just washing out of me all the junk I've had inside, and it feels so good just to be able to say "I'm sorry."' When he had finished I said to him, 'Go in peace. The Lord has put away all your sins.'

I repeated those words and told him to listen to them again. He threw his hands up in the air and said, 'I feel new. I feel wonderful! I feel released!' He went back to his psychiatrist and asked him why he hadn't told him about this twelve years ago! The psychiatrist called me back and offered to share his fee with me! As a result of the man's sharing his experience, the psychiatrist came to church and told me, 'With all my years of training in psychotherapy I can really help people understand their problems, come to terms with their problems, and live with their problems. But I've never seen anybody get rid of them in a way that is so cleansing.'

Don't misunderstand: therapy can be helpful. It is like dropping a dozen rotten eggs on the floor. Therapy can help us identify that there are eggs there, that they are broken and smelly. It can help us step over them and get on with our lives. The problem is that we can always recollect the smell! But when we admit the fact that we've really screwed up, it brings us before God in such a way that God is able to say to us, 'I have cleaned up the mess. It is no longer there for you to pay attention to. You are now free to get on with your life, not live with the mess, but be free of it.'

As a result of Adam and Eve's disobedience (the 'Fall'), we find ourselves in their position: in bondage to ourselves, to our experience, to our life. We hide, we are shameful, we run away, our hearts are broken. There is something in us that propels us in the wrong direction. Theology calls it 'original sin'. It is that tendency in all of us to move away from God.

Part of us longs for God, but a bigger part pulls us away. If you leave a plant in a window, you'll find it always leans towards the sun. It is attracted toward that which has the biggest pull on it. There is something in us that leans away from God and toward other things which appear to be very attractive, but in our best moments we know that they are not what we really want. Given this pull what are we to do? To whom can we turn?

Who will deliver me from this body of death?

St Paul, in his Letter to the Romans, says, 'Who will deliver me from this body of death?' (7:24). It is a plea. On Palm Sunday, when we wave our palm branches and sing 'Hosanna', we are not giving praise. 'Hosanna' comes from a root word meaning 'save'. Save us! We are asking: 'Who will begin to take care of that inner me that runs away and puts false make-up on my soul so that I can look good? Who will deliver me from this pool of sadness?'

God cannot ever really touch us in this way, until we are able to rightly diagnose our malady—until we realize that we are running away from him, that we have a lot in our lives that needs changing and saving, and we do not know what to do about it. We can come to church five times a week and try to put an ecclesiastical band-aid on top of our wounds, but it will not take care of the hurt, until the proper diagnosis is given and the proper remedy looked for.

All through the Scriptures you see this basic understanding that comes right out of the book of Genesis: we were created for a relationship with God, there was a proper order to that relationship, we decided we wanted to be at the centre instead of God, and therefore God said 'I'll let you go.'

God will always look for us, but he'll also let us go our own way, and leave us with the consequences of our independence. The whole of the Old Testament tells of God's searching for us, to bring us back to him; and then, if we can understand what our malady (our 'dis-ease') is, and accept the fact that we are people in need of a 'physician' to cure it, the coming of Jesus into the world begins to make sense. It is not a teacher, or a good man that we need, it is not a radical reformer that we need—it is, in fact, somebody who will save us and heal us and enable us to live rightly. That is what the Bible says Jesus wants to do for each one of us.

CHAPTER 4

HOW DOES GOD DEAL WITH OUR NEEDS?

Once we realize we are in need of a cure, we must begin to consider what, if anything, God has done to respond to the sense of dis-ease or brokenheartedness in us.

God understands our quandry and has been working since the beginning of creation to draw us back to himself. The whole of Scripture is really the story of God's struggle with us. In almost all world religions, with the exception of Judaism, the whole focus has to do with human beings trying to reach God—through meditation, through denial of our own life in one way or another, or through obeying a certain number of laws. For a Muslim, for instance, there is a prescribed list of things that he or she is expected to do in order to reach a state of blessedness. It's as if to say, 'If only I do these things, then maybe God will find me acceptable.'

This is a condition that often invades the Christian churches, too. It's part of our middle class myth that acceptability is really important. 'Manners maketh the man,' is the motto of one of the most respected preparatory schools in the United States. There is no question that manners are important, but manners are not enough, nor is being 'nice'. How often do we hear someone described as a 'good Christian', when what is really meant is that the person is nice or kind, or that they do a great deal of good. The understanding is that what we do makes us acceptable to God.

The Bible talks about God seeking us out. For instance, God promised Abraham and Sarah that he would be their God and they would be his people. They would walk closely together if they would trust him as their God. Later, God met Moses on Mount Sinai and gave him the Ten Commandments. These were not meant to be laws to hit people over the head with; they were given by the grace of God so that we might know how to live in fellowship with him. The problems of people in the Old Testament were caused by their either being too rigid or too lax in their obedience to the law. Is God someone who's behind us all the time looking over our shoulder, trying to catch us out? Does God 'keep score?' Is that who he really is?

There is a tension in the Old Testament. God is outlining the things that will bring us closer to him, but he is also telling us there are some house rules we need to follow. There are consequences to our walking away from God. If we don't live in accordance with God's will, we become spiritually sick. We find ourselves caught between what God wants and what we want to do, and then we really get ourselves in trouble.

Sigmund Freud had a wonderful way of describing the situation we get ourselves into. He told us we have an 'ego', that which makes us who we are. The ego, on one side, is driven by what we want to do, pushing us towards our desire. He calls this the 'libido'. It says, 'Forget the rules, live for yourself with all the gusto you can.'

On the other hand, there is the 'super ego', which we would call the 'conscience'. It is that part of us which keeps us in check. The libido and the super ego fight it out constantly. According to Freud, we have these drives within us telling us to satisfy our wants, just like Adam and Eve in the book of Genesis when the voice said, 'Go ahead and eat the fruit; who is God to tell you not to?' Then there is the other voice which says, 'But, hold on, you shouldn't be doing this. You should be doing things that are pleasing to God.' And we are caught in the middle. Freud said that these two drives push together like a vice, with us in the middle, and we don't know how to free ourselves from it. He really asks the question that Paul asks, 'Who will deliver me from this body of death?' (Romans 7:24).

We move away from God and yet he draws us back. We are torn between these two poles. That is the human condition—and very often it feels like bondage.

The atonement

How does God answer that problem? How does he break the impasse in our lives? The Scriptures, beyond diagnosing our malady, tell us that we are not able to break the impasse ourselves: God must do it for us. In the Old Testament, a ritual was developed to deal with this. Most of us react against its primitive nature, but rituals often penetrate to a deeper level in our souls than we think possible. This ritual took place on the day called the Day of Atonement, Yom Kippur.

In order to be able to achieve reconciliation with God animal sacrifices were made. Although this is hard for us to understand in our culture, this is what would have happened. People came to Jerusalem with their family and brought with them a goat and a spotless lamb. They would have taken the goat to the outskirts of Jerusalem, laid their hands on the goat's head and transferred the sins of the past year onto it. The goat would then be sent off into the wilderness (that's where the phrase 'scapegoat' comes from). There was a transfer of the sins from their own life onto the goat.

It was also believed that the offence of people against God was so great that the punishment was 'capital', a death sentence. God presented an alternative to this sentence: he would receive a substitute whose life could be offered, a spotless lamb. The lamb was taken to the Temple, hands were laid on it again, the guilt placed on the lamb, and its throat was then cut. The 'lifeblood' was collected and given to the high priest.

The temple was divided into various sections, and the most holy section was called the 'Holy of Holies', where it was believed that God dwelt behind a veil. Nobody, except the high priest, was allowed into the presence of God, because everybody was unclean and full of sin. The high priest would go into the Holy of Holies and he would pour the lamb's blood onto a table (called the 'mercy seat') and pray that God would find the offering acceptable. If the priest did not die (meaning the offering was found acceptable), he would then return to the people and declare that their sins were forgiven. There was great rejoicing. The problem with this system was that it had to be endlessly repeated, year after year.

Another problem with this animal sacrifice was that there was never any sense that individuals had any power over the sin in their own lives. They did not have any sense of direct access to God. Their sins were forgiven but their fundamental relationship with God did not change. They would have to go through it all again the next year.

As we look back on the quandary of how we deal with

our own sinfulness we have to ask, 'How does God deal with the reality of sin in our lives?' God's quandary is different than ours. Sin is an offence to God as well as to those we have sinned against. There is a holiness and righteousness in God which cannot be bypassed (we would like to think it can, but this is not so). On the other hand, God loves us so much that he doesn't wish to leave us in a state of condemnation. So, in the New Testament, we have the coming of Jesus. The central purpose of Jesus' coming into the world was to restore our relationship with God: for that to take place, he had to go to Jerusalem to die.

When Jesus asked, 'Who do you say that I am?', Peter answered, 'You are the Christ.' Jesus responded by saying, in effect, 'Now that you know who I am, this is what I'm going to do. I will go to Jerusalem where I will be betrayed and where I will be crucified, to give my life as a ransom for many.' Peter tells him he mustn't do this, perhaps appalled that this should happen to Jesus. And Jesus responds, 'Get behind me, Satan!' (Mark 8:31–33). Poor Peter didn't know what to make of it! But Jesus was trying to say to him, 'Listen, you don't understand. I've come to die. I've not come to be a great moral teacher, I've not come to be a great religious leader, I've not even come to set up a church. I've come into this world to be able to make it possible for people to be reconciled to God.' The way in which that could happen was to take that image of sacrifice from the Old Testament and to accept that a substitute had to be sacrificed for the world, once and for all.

In the Gospel of John, we read that the first time John the Baptist saw Jesus, he said, 'Behold, the Lamb of God, who takes away the sin of the world!' (1:29). There is a part of us that listens to this and a part that is repulsed by it. It is so primitive, so unpleasant, but the whole purpose for Jesus' coming was, in fact, to offer himself as a sacrifice for us—to die for us. Remember back in Genesis, God said that 'if you eat of the tree of knowledge of good and evil you will die'. We have seen that God was not only talking about physical death, but also about spiritual death. Jesus came to take that death upon himself, on the cross. He takes our estrangement from God, our sinfulness, and breaks the grip of that vice which holds us. Jesus' death on the cross is not an accident. God does not wish to let us go, so he himself comes to pay the penalty that we should receive. He takes our death upon himself. The cross takes that part of ourselves which we just can't live with anymore and gives it to God. And he gives us back his own life; that is what the resurrection is about.

If we were in a court, and God was the judge, he would leave his judgement seat, stand next to us in the dock and say to us, 'If that is the punishment, I will bear it for you.' Karl Barth, a great twentieth century theologian, calls this 'the judge, judged in our place.' God says, I will forgive you and cleanse you, and I will give you the strength and power to live the life I have called you to. I will give you a new heart—mine. I will give you new life.' Our response is to accept that or reject it. That's essentially what the New Testament is about.

Jesus not only came to show us what God is like, but also to reconcile us to God so that we are able to have a relationship with him. We cannot do it for ourselves. We cannot earn it, and we certainly do not deserve it. He pours out his lifeblood, goes to the Father, and asks: 'Is this acceptable?' And the Father says, 'Yes.'

While he is on the cross Jesus says 'It is finished', (John 19:30). The original Greek word for 'finished' means both 'that which is transacted is fulfilled', and 'paid in full.' Jesus says to the Father, 'I have paid their debt.' We do not have to carry the burden of our lives anymore. He has done that for us. After saying this, Jesus dies with a shout. It is over. It is complete. 'It is finished.' Immediately 'the veil of the temple was rent in twain from the top to the bottom' (Mark 15:38 AV). Can you imagine what that means? No longer is God hidden behind a veil. He is now accessible to everybody. The sin that has kept people from him, symbolized by that veil, is now pulled apart. Anyone can come into the presence of God because of what Christ has done. Fear of God is lost: all the symbolism in the story is about that.

In Christian baptism we are taken into the water, put under and brought up again; it is a cleansing and a new birth. It is like putting our old lives into the grave and rising again, all because of what Christ has done through his death and resurrection. He has paid the penalty once and for all, but we do not benefit from it until we, like those people with the goat and the lamb, lay our sins on Christ and give our lives to him. He gives us back himself, his life. It is really a transaction that happens. As Ezekiel the prophet said, God takes the old 'heart of stone' out of us and gives us what the Old Testament calls a 'heart of flesh'. We are spiritually alive because he comes and puts back into us his very life.

One of our parish leaders is a surgeon who does heart transplants. He takes out the old diseased heart and puts a new one into the patient, connects the blood vessels together and then jolts the heart to start it. Every time he does this, he wonders whether the heart is going to start. Almost every time it does, and he watches as the vessels begin to work and life is pumped back into the body. The person takes on new life because of the donor who, in essence, died for them. That is a little like what Christ did. He died for us, he gives us his new heart, and his life begins to work in us.

'You must be born again'

The phrase 'born again', which terrifies many traditional churchgoers, comes from John chapter 3, where Nicodemus, a learned man, came to Jesus. He asked Jesus how he could receive the life which he had heard Jesus talking about, and Jesus replies, 'You must be born again.' (John 3:7 NIV). Nicodemus takes him literally and asks how he can return to his mother's womb. Jesus explains that unless he is born from above—unless he has the life which comes from God—he will not be able to have the life that God intends. Nicodemus went away pondering, but as you read the rest of the Gospel you discover that Nicodemus eventually became a follower of Jesus.

The same is true for us: unless we are 'born again' we cannot find that abundant life which God gives us in Christ. That is the only way it can happen. When we see what Christ has done for us on the Cross it becomes the place where our faith and our life take on real meaning.

How do we respond?

We need to be able, at some point, to admit that we are not living the life God wants us to lead. Our lives may be good or bad, but it's not what God wants. We must acknowledge that we can't fix our own lives, and accept what Christ has done for us. We need to be reconciled to God through Christ. That is what it means to 'receive Christ into our life'. We have to take the first step. If we give our life to God we will be able to hear him say, 'I receive you; you are my beloved daughter, my beloved son, in whom I am well pleased. And I give you back my life, the life you see in Jesus.'

Some of us may already have been baptized, and that is a relationship with God that has begun and continued in our lives; but it is one which must be ratified by our own commitment to him. Some of us have said to God that we want to be able to trust him and walk with him, but we are not really sure that we have that reconciliation with God that he has promised. In order to do that, we will need to say a prayer of commitment to Christ, and I give one to use at the end of this chapter. If you feel God is calling you to do this, please pray it. If God is dealing with you, it is important to be able to say 'Yes'.

This happened to me in 1977, six years after I was ordained. At that time, I had to be able to process all of my life in my brain and I found myself needing to think it all through, making sure I was in charge, knowing how everything worked. I was like a child taking something apart in a corner. I heard somebody talking about Christ in the way I have mentioned and it cut into my heart like a knife. I resisted thinking about it for days! I was aware of it even at night!

C. S. Lewis, in his book *Surprised by Joy*, has a great line about this, discussing his own conversion: 'Man's search for God makes about as much sense as the mouse's search for the cat!' He described his own conversion, in the Trinity Term of 1929, 'feeling . . .

the steady, unrelenting approach of Him whom I so earnestly desired not to meet. That which I greatly feared had at last come upon me . . . I gave in, and admitted that God was God, and knelt and prayed: perhaps, that night, the most dejected and reluctant convert in all England.'

When I finally got to make a commitment to Christ, I'm sure there was a huge cosmic sigh of relief as if God said: 'This woman has asked so many questions!' But I have since learned that God is with us in our struggle. I told God I had not understood the fulness of what he had done and that I didn't have the proper words with which to say it, but that I wanted to give my life to him in a total and complete way. After this prayer, I picked up the phone and called a priest friend. 'This is wonderful,' he said, and he sent me a card saying 'Happy Birthday'! He understood that this was the day of my rebirth.

So, if you are ready to do the same, I invite you to say the following prayer. You are saying to God: 'Here's my life. I can't please you. I can't please myself. I can't please anybody else.' God is saying: 'That's alright, come just as you are.'

Prayer

Lord Jesus, you know my heart better than I do. You know the sin in my life, you know the things that I do and the things that I don't do. You know the ways in which I have tried to avoid you and even the ways in which I have tried to reach you. I find myself longing to know you, but I know I cannot unless you make it possible. So I give you thanks Lord, that from the very beginning of the universe you had me in mind, and came into this world to make it possible for me to know God and to live for him.

Lord Jesus, I give you my life now, all of it, the good and the bad; and like those ancient people I lay my sin upon you and accept that in your death you made the perfect offering for my life. I now receive you and all of your life into my life. I receive you as my Saviour and rescuer, the one who will deliver me from this body of death. And I give you thanks. Help me, Lord Jesus, to be able to acknowledge you as my Saviour and not to be afraid to rejoice in that. Help me to live for you. I give you thanks for your great love to me. Amen.

If you have said this prayer and meant it, there is great rejoicing in heaven!

CHAPTER 5

THE CALL TO RESPONSE AND COMMITMENT

In the last chapter we talked about how Jesus meets the needs of our human condition. Perhaps you have not been able to make a commitment to Christ yet. That is alright. It is important that we come to a relationship with Christ in our own time and in our own way, and anybody who is not able to do that yet should not feel left out of the rest of this book. Ask your questions, sort things out, God will stay with you.

When we turn over our lives to Christ and he begins to give his life to us, things don't always change immediately. In fact it can be a little discouraging when we see some of our 'old life' still present. If you look at a tree in the autumn when all the leaves have died, there's nearly always one dry, brown leaf left hanging from a branch and you can't figure out how it manages to stay there. The Christian life is a little like that. We are dead to the old life because Christ has taken it away from us, but there are still dead leaves hanging on, things from the old life that haven't fallen off the tree yet. But it's important to realize that those old leaves are dead. The power of our old way of life to define and destroy us is gone, but that doesn't mean we change completely overnight. I still yell at bad drivers and I am still selfish, even though I've been a Christian a long time. But the fact is that the old life is not who we are anymore. Christ defines who we are now. Instead of being bound to the old life, turn it over to him. It's like a leaf hanging on, but it's dead.

We spend all of our earthly life working out our relationship with Christ. Each day something will crop up and we'll think it's our old ways calling us again. Instead of panicking and seeing the issue as something that will destroy us, we should think of it as something we need to work on. Christ gives us power over the dead leaves which are hanging onto our lives, but we have the responsibility to deal with them as they come up. What we are used to doing is to focus on areas of our own choosing, but the Lord says, 'No, this is the area I want to deal with.' This can be painful. These are the times when we have to trust the fact that Jesus has transacted something and we have to start acting on it. There are times when we have to act on what we know to be true and then wait for our feelings to follow.

Steam trains have an engine, a coal truck and a caboose. Very often the engine which is driving our lives is our feelings. Behind it is our faith, being dragged along. But the way in which the Christian life works best is to have the engine be the facts, the givens of the Christian faith; our faith becomes the coal truck feeding the engine; and the caboose becomes our feelings following along behind. The train only really moves when we trust the facts as we hear them and put our faith in them. We need to learn to act on what, in our better moments, we believe to be true. During the most difficult periods, is when God is most active. He's saying, 'Are you trusting me when I do not seem to be present?'

Sharing your faith

It is important to share your faith. I made a very personal commitment to Christ six years after I was ordained. It was a major theological shift for me as well as a personal experience, but I only told a couple of people. A while later I was going to a seminary to speak, having been invited by one of our bishops to go there. I arrived on the seminary grounds and was horrified to see posters on trees all over the place saying 'Come hear Carol Anderson talk about her conversion!' I was angry and scared! I had shifted gears profoundly in my own life, but the last thing in the world I wanted to be known as was one of those people who go around 'witnessing'.

Not only was my conversion advertized all over the campus, but when I arrived in the room where I was to speak a large number of the student body was there. At this time I had become well-known in the national church because of the women's ordination controversy, so I had expected more than a handful of listeners, but the trustees were there as well, having cancelled a board meeting to come! There were also a number of bishops. They were all packed into this room waiting for me to talk, and they all had a quizzical look on their faces, as if to say, 'What has happened to you?' I remember staring at the bishop who had set me up for this, and if I'd had a gun I would have cheerfully shot him! Picture yourself having somebody set you up to talk about something so utterly personal in front of hundreds of your colleagues. That's the situation I found myself in!

So I faced the crowd and began stammering. I told them I thought I was there to talk about one thing and they wanted to hear me talk about something else, at which point the bishop interrupted me and said, 'Tell us what happened to you!' Right out loud! Everyone was straining forward, looking at me, trying to figure out what I was going to say. I started talking very haltingly and obviously didn't say enough because the bishop interrupted again and said, 'Tell us what happened to you!' You can imagine how I felt inside! I was so embarrassed. I staggered on as best I could and people began asking me very pointed questions. I finally managed to finish telling the story.

Afterwards people approached me and said, 'I don't understand what's happened to you. Is this a change of politics?' They thought I'd become a fundamentalist or some other label they could give me. I fled from the campus to the aeroplane and back to New York as fast as I could. I would have sat on the plane's wing, if necessary, to get out of there!

By the time the plane landed in New York the anger I felt for the bishop was completely dissipated and I found that something had sprung loose inside of me. I can't tell you what it was, but by the time I was in the terminal building I felt much more comfortable talking about my faith. I went on to talk to other people about these things and found many more were intrigued, too. But it was being forced to put my experience into words which started this whole process of sharing. Even though the situation had been an appalling introduction to telling my story, it had done the trick. It pushed me off home base and got me talking publicly about my faith.

Wherever you are in your faith, it is important to realize that it is not just an emotional transaction but a conscious turning over of one's life to Christ, and it is important to be able to share this with others. That doesn't mean you have to stand on a street corner, buttonhole people and ask, 'Are you saved?' You don't have to be a theologian or know all the answers.

One of my favourite stories in the New Testament is Jesus' healing of a blind man (John 9:1–34). The religious leaders came to question the man afterwards and asked him what had happened to him, what Jesus had said and done. The blind man replied simply, 'I don't know, all I know is that I was blind and now I see.' It was his testimony, the truth as he saw it.

In the same way, we can tell people of our experience with Jesus and that God is involved with our lives. We can tell people we believe in Jesus and that something life-changing happened on the cross. We don't have to say much more to anyone than that. You will find something released in you when you begin to do so. The Spirit of God begins to free us up as we learn to articulate our commitment more and more.

I have never, ever seen an Episcopalian become obnoxious about sharing their faith! D. L. Moody, who was a great evangelist at the turn of the century said, 'Half-filled glasses do not overflow!' I want to encourage you to try talking to others about your faith! God will confirm what has happened to you when you begin to share your story. Don't worry about offending people. Don't try to sound like a preacher; just try to be honest about who you are and share it.

Resurrection life

What is our new life like? When we discussed Jesus' question, 'Who do you say that I am,' Peter had the right answer. Shortly thereafter, when Jesus was arrested, Peter denied that he had ever known him. Peter was absent during much of Jesus' trial and crucifixion. He was off hiding somewhere. Yet after the resurrection, Peter was sought out by Jesus, very personally taken aside by him, and, in one of the most poignant passages in the New Testament, Jesus asks him if he loves him (John 21:15–19). Can you imagine Peter's feelings, hanging his head in shame, afraid to even come into Jesus' presence anymore? Jesus asks him the same question three times and Peter's answers become more and more insistent. 'You know that I love you.' Jesus gives him back his ministry and says 'Feed my sheep, Feed my people.'

In the book of Acts we see Peter taking up leadership in the first church because he really believed that the Jesus who died on the cross was now alive and living in him and in others. And that church grew. On the day of Pentecost three thousand people were added to the church! In the first hundred years after the resurrection of Jesus the church grew to a hundred thousand members! And all that tremendous growth was based on people just like us!

What would happen if we became like those first Christians? The life that Jesus had shown the early church when he was on the earth was now living in them. It's called 'resurrection life'. What happens when that life begins to work in us?

Power over sin in our lives

The first thing that resurrection life gives us is power over sin in our lives. It means that the force which drives us to do the things we should not, or do not want to do, is no longer all-powerful. It doesn't mean that we're not tempted. It doesn't mean that you and I, until the day we die, are not going to get annoyed at the way people cut us off in traffic! But it does mean that we have a power we can call on to help us to stop doing the things we don't want to. Christ will break the power of those things in our lives that go against his way. He has power over sin and he puts that power in us.

There is one particular person whom I just can't stand. I like almost everybody, and I can get along with almost anybody, but this man is one of those people who when he walks into a room brings the worst things out in me, instantly. If he opens his mouth, I want to say nasty things to him. If he says, 'Carol, you look wonderful today,' I want to reply, 'Drop dead!' He pushes all my buttons at once and has for years!

Recently I was at a meeting we were both a part of. I decided I had to deal with this problem. I'd prayed that the Lord would really give me the power to love this man. I arrived at the meeting, saw him and could feel all the old animosity bubbling up. I wanted to put a gag on my mouth! 'Lord', I prayed, 'give me the power to deal with this.' Clear as a bell I could hear a little voice in my conscience telling me, 'You act lovingly towards him and I will give you the power to follow through.' I asked for plan B, but it never came!

That is how God operates in our lives; he awakens our conscience and points us towards what is right. We become increasingly fine-tuned to the ways of God. God will give us the power to triumph over these problems but we have to take the first step. Once we do, he will come right along with us. Sometimes we say, 'Lord, take this away from me,' and nothing happens. We wonder what God's up to, why he doesn't hurry up, but what God is really saying to us is, 'If you desire to be my follower and you know what is right to do, start acting on it in obedience and my Spirit will come and help you with it.' I've found that to be true, again and again, in my own life. What God wants to see is the intention of our hearts. Once we move in the right direction he will be there with us.

A man was complaining to me about his wife, who was driving him crazy. I said to him, 'Why don't you start behaving lovingly towards her and see what happens?' He replied, 'I don't want to!' And therein lay the dilemma. I suggested he ask the Lord to help him act lovingly towards her, and although he initially resisted, he decided to try it. He called me a while later, told me he'd started to act that way and that the funniest thing had happened. At first his wife had said, 'What's the matter with you?'

'Nothing, absolutely nothing,' he replied.

'Yes there is,' she said, 'what have you done wrong?' She thought he had done something and was trying to make up for it!

He told me, 'You know this is really beginning to work. If I just get up in the morning and really try to be encouraging and supportive, it's as if another thing kicks in and makes it happen.'

That is what it means to have power over sin. When we are left to our own devices we have only ourselves to rely on, but in the Christian life God gives us his power to draw on. He keeps working with us on our problems. It's not, 'Lord come and take this away from me', nor is it us trying to make it on our own, it's a combination of the two. We know what we are supposed to do, we step out and God helps us fulfil it. We then begin to experience what resurrection life is all about.

That is what happened to the early disciples. They started to do the things they'd seen Jesus doing when he was walking with them on earth. Who in the world would call Peter to be their spiritual leader? But look what happened to him. Jesus built his entire Church upon Peter's leadership. If Jesus can do that with Peter, there's nothing he can't do with any of us! That is what is so exciting about resurrection life! It is a life with power over sin.

Death, where is thy victory?

The second thing that happens in resurrection life is that death no longer has any grip on us. Death, that sense of things always falling apart, is a by-product of a world out of relationship with God. Remember that God said if Adam and Eve ate of the tree of the knowledge of good and evil they would perish? Spiritual death is reversed in Christ. Not only did he break the power of death when he was raised from the dead, but he also broke the fear of dying in us. We can actually become people who are hopeful—hopeful in situations where the world would think no hope is possible. Even if we physically die, it is not the end of our life, we live in Christ forever.

When I was in my second parish in New York City I would go out occasionally and visit a local drug dealer who kept me informed about the neighbourhood. One afternoon we were walking up Amsterdam Avenue when we came upon a couple of drug dealers, shooting at one another! There were bullets flying everywhere, very close to where I was! The man who was with me said, 'Get out of here!' But for some reason I replied, 'No, I'm not leaving.' He said, 'You'll be shot if you don't get out of here!'

Instead of being frightened at the prospect, I found myself absolutely calm in the midst of all this chaos, even though I am just as much a coward as the next person. When I finally realized that I could, indeed, get myself killed, I kept saying over and over in my mind, 'Death has no sting. Don't worry about it. There are people who are getting hurt here and somebody has got to stop this.' I moved away from the wall and waded out into the middle of it all. I yelled, 'Stop this!' To my amazement they all stopped! I had my clerical collar on and hoped they would think twice about shooting a priest! Despite the fact that I couldn't be sure of this I really had a sense of calm, and it was more than just bravado on my part: my faith came to the rescue and said, 'Don't be afraid of death.'

If you've ever been to the funeral of someone who really was a committed Christian, you'll have noticed an enormous amount of joy in the service. Of course, there is sadness; people cry because they're going to miss somebody; but the hymns are hymns of joy and gladness, of resurrection and hope, just about the most exciting texts imaginable. That type of funeral is such a celebration it is almost a party! Even though the family knows a person has physically died and misses him or her deeply, they know that their loved one is living in the presence of God.

When we live in the resurrection, death does not have the power to hold us anymore, either ultimately or in the daily business of living. The secret is to find a calm centre in the midst of the 'death' that hits us day to day. Sometimes we ask God to change the situation, but what God does instead is to change us in the situation, rather than change the circumstances.

I know a wonderful man for whom this is true. One of his sons had been brain-damaged in a car accident, another son had committed suicide at junior college three months later, and he and his wife had not recovered from these shocks. I was very quiet while he told me his story. What could I say? He turned and looked at me and said, 'You know, the strangest thing is that I feel my faith has strengthened more than ever before. Not that I don't get depressed at times. I went to a psychiatrist because I couldn't deal with my family's grief, let alone my own. Yet something has been released in me that makes my faith more real today that it ever was before. It hasn't given me my son back, and it hasn't healed my other boy, but I have come to know a power I would never have experienced otherwise. Despite this tragedy, I really feel that death has no power over me.'

There is a power in the death and resurrection of Jesus which tells us that, although death still is strong in the world, Christ will give us his resurrection life; and that, if we draw upon him, we will have joy even if everything else falls apart. As we grow day by day and week by week in relation to Christ, we discover that there are situations in life which are seemingly random and meaningless, but in the midst of which we will, nevertheless, have joy.

God will give us the power that we need to do difficult and risky things. Why do Christians move into the difficult areas of the world for social welfare? Or work with the poor in Calcutta? Who, historically, are the ones who started hospitals, improved prisons, ended slavery? More Christians have died for their faith and commitment in the twentieth century than in all other previous centuries! Resurrection life is life lived without fear of death. Resurrection life is rejoicing in new life.

At some of our worship services we read from a book called *Lesser Feasts and Fasts*, which examines the lives of saints throughout the centuries. We read stories about people who went to Eton and Cambridge, were ordained, went off to some South Sea island or Africa and after only a few months were killed. I used to think this was not right—what was accomplished by 'throwing away' a life like that? Gradually I realized that a Christian's life is not measured in years but in faithfulness. These saints would go to some far off place and be murdered, and in the way they died the people saw in them something which they had never seen before: people who cared for them even as they were being killed.

The missionaries who came after were the ones who could actually do the work of bringing people to Christ because of the witness of those deaths. These saints had short lives but they made a difference. In a Christian's life that is not wasteful because faithfulness and witness are so important. When we are not afraid of putting our lives on the line, when we are not afraid of situations which may cause us trouble or stress, and when we realize that there is resurrection life at work in us, we are capable of doing what others wouldn't dare to do. That is really quite extraordinary.

Satan is conquered

Satan is that personal spiritual force at work in the universe opposing the things of God. Some believe in him, some don't. Jesus believed in him, and so do I. Satan was the one who thought he could destroy Jesus by having him put to death. When Jesus was resurrected from death, Satan's power to undo and destroy things in this world was no longer total. This does not mean he cannot still hurt people's lives. Satan often whispers in our ears, 'You don't really believe all this about Jesus do you? You don't really think you're going to change?' But, when we belong to Christ, that evil power in the universe does not have ultimate sway over us. I have seen people who have been destroyed by drugs and the hellish life of degradation that goes along with that, people who have seemed hopeless, transformed by the power of Jesus. Satan's grip has been broken.

What does this mean in everyday life?

Seeing ourselves through God's eyes

One of the first things that happens when we commit our lives to Christ is that we realize we are defined by what he says about us, not by what we say about ourselves or by what the world says. We need to know what that means.

When we look in the mirror in the morning how do we feel? When we are really depressed, what do we think about ourselves? I have moments when I say to myself, 'Carol, you're not going to get anywhere in life. You're not going to amount to anything. Your work is fruitless. And you'll never lose weight, to boot.' How do we describe ourselves in those moments? We don't always like what we see.

What does Christ say about us? He says we are a beloved daughter, a beloved son. He says we are adopted into his family and have been given the rights to everything he has. He says that he died for us. If we were the only ones in the universe who needed saving, he would still have died for us. We are the wonder of God's creation, the joy of his life. Jesus sees in us something extraordinary.

I've spent some time walking around our pre-school and I've seen the way our three or four-year-olds are cherished. The teachers make them feel as if they are very important—not self-centred, but valued. No question is out of bounds. No child causing a fight is chastised, but the teacher will sit down with them and work out what caused it. When they leave for their next school they feel that they are worthwhile. I think that's a parable of how God deals with us. He treats us like those teachers do; he 'sits' with us, takes time with us, and lets us know that he wants to love and encourage us. He wants to move us along in just the way a good teacher would do. He calls us into his new life by loving us. Jesus sees what we can be. This is a whole new way of building our self-esteem, not by saying to ourselves, 'I am wonderful', but by his loving us the way we are. 'Beloved son, beloved daughter in whom I am well-pleased,'—that's what he says about us. That is what God said to Jesus at the time of his baptism.

One of the stories that best illustrates this to me is from the play *Bus Stop*. One of the characters, Cherry, has had a pretty seedy, turbulent life, and a guy named Beau falls in love with her. She is petrified that Beau will find out about her past, so she tells him that she's lived a very bad life and that she's not worthy of him. Beau responds by saying, 'I love you the way you are. I don't care how you got that way.'

God says that Christ has given himself for us and that he cherishes us because of that. He will love us as we are, and that brings us the freedom to start acting the way we should, to become the kind of person God sees in us. Christ starts working in our souls and gives us his love. He restores the image of God in us that has become blurred by our living apart from him, then we begin to become like him.

When I first started college I was quite shy and introverted, afraid of speaking and afraid of making a fool of myself. Only since I have begun to realize who I am in Christ have I been able to stand in the pulpit and go about my ministry. If you had told me twenty-five years ago that I would be preaching in church on a Sunday morning I would not have believed you. It is only because he has worked into me not only a sense of who I am, but what I am called to do, that I can undertake this.

Many of us grow up in families where, unintentionally, we are not told we are loved. Much is expected of us, but there is little overt sense of our worth expressed. These feelings of inferiority begin to stick to our insides and we never quite believe that we are accepted. But Christ says, not only are we accepted, but we are also cherished. Our self-esteem begins to be repaired, and we start to feel loved.

The power to forgive

We hang onto a lot of hurt in our lives. There are moments when God will tell us quite clearly to let go of it. In Lewis Smede's book, *Forgive and Forget* he tells the story of Cynthia Sewell, a widow with a seventeen year old son. He was riding a motor scooter and was killed by a drunk driver. The driver was caught and taken to court. Cynthia hated this man passionately. The bitterness that she felt for the taking away of her son, who was so special, so good, and had such a promising future, was intense. She wanted the driver to die.

Cynthia was a Christian, and this bitter hatred didn't square with her faith. She went to see her minister and told him she couldn't go on living this way. The clergyman told her to forgive the driver. 'I won't,' she replied. She felt her hatred was like one of those double-stick scotch tapes—the kind that sticks to one finger as soon as it's pulled off the other, then it gets onto your clothes and cannot be got rid of. Cynthia's hatred stuck to her, no matter what. She had been saying to God over and over that she wouldn't forgive this man. She realized that her bitterness was eating up her life; for two years every conscious moment had been spent thinking about the driver and her son's death. Finally she realized she could move from 'I won't forgive him' to 'I can't forgive him' and asked the Lord for help. When she gave God permission to do something about it, he took the hatred away from her. She's never forgotten what happened to her son, but God gave her the power to forgive that man. Is that something we can do in our natural lives? I don't think so. That's part of our new life in Christ. It's the Spirit of God working in us that enables us to forgive like that.

The life we have in Christ is an adventure that will not be simple, easy or dull. It will take us in all kinds of directions. We will be doing things we never thought we would do, saying things we never thought we would say. Being a Christian—a disciple, a follower of Christ— is not a panacea which creates immediate happiness. Any religion that claims that it makes life perfect is selling us a cheap bill of goods. But when Christ comes to live in us, we will have a life we would not want to trade, even when the tough times come along. Christ gives us a quality of relationship with God we will never have experienced before. The adventures we will have in prayer, in study of Scripture, in witness and in life itself will, day by day, show us the reality of God's power and his love. I have been a Christian for years now, I have had the most extraordinary journey, and I would not trade one day of that for my old way of life.

Jesus loves us

How do we sum up the Christian life? I went to a conference on evangelism, which was quite academic. I listened to all the sophisticated talk, but found myself reminded of a story about Karl Barth. He wrote the most finely argued theology you would ever want to read, called *Church Dogmatics* (if you ever have insomnia you can borrow my copy!). Divinity students would flock to the University of Basel to study with him. He puffed on a pipe and had a great mane of hair. An interviewer from *Time Magazine* once asked him to sum up his theology. The response? Barth took the pipe out of his mouth and began to sing the children's hymn, 'Jesus loves me, this I know, for the Bible tells me so.'

Your faith has to start there, in a recognition that God loves us. God loves all of us. There are no exceptions. No matter what our past is, no matter what others may say, this is the fundamental witness of the Christian faith. God loves us and in order to win us back to himself, in Christ went to the cross and was raised from the dead to be able to live in us and through us, so that we might be witnesses to his life in a world that is caught in the jaws of death. Behind all of the complexities and under the surface there is a world longing to hear that Jesus loves us. That is the great joy about witnessing to the Christian faith.

CHAPTER 6

THE KINGDOM LIFE

We come to the last piece of the puzzle we have been
putting together. We have talked about who Jesus is
and why he came; we've discussed commitment to him
and how he works in our lives. Now I want to look at
why it is that we are reconciled to God. It is not just for
us to have the intimate relationship with God that was
intended by God in creation; it is not just for the
forgiveness of our own sins and the redemption of our
own lives: we are rescued by Christ *from* something and
for a purpose. We are rescued from an old life and called
to a different style of living. The life Jesus calls us to is
the Kingdom life. He changes our hearts and minds so
that we can live in a different way, not only on a personal
level, but in the world. He is turning us toward a new
way of understanding and living.

The Gospel of Mark, chapter one, verses 14 and 15
records the very beginning of the ministry of Jesus. The
chapter starts with John the Baptist who proclaimed the
coming of the Messiah.

Now after John was arrested, Jesus came into Galilee,
preaching the gospel of God, and saying, 'The time is
fulfilled, and the kingdom of God is at hand; repent, and
believe in the gospel.'

The whole essence of Jesus' preaching was the Kingdom of God, meaning the reign or rule of God. The life that God intended from the beginning of time was lost in the Fall of Adam and Eve. In Mark's Gospel, that life is being reclaimed by Jesus. He is talking about a spiritual kingdom, not a political or military one. The very first thing Jesus does in his public ministry is to proclaim the Kingdom of God.

Imagine if I became the potentate of Beverly Hills! I would be able to establish a new order in town. That is what Jesus did, but the order he established was the visible manifestation of the things of God, a way of life that had been hidden, clouded and lost for centuries. We can glimpse bits and pieces of it in the words of the prophets in the Old Testament, but it came to light in Jesus' life and ministry.

A closer look at the passage quoted above shows that in the Greek language there are two words for 'time'. One of them is *Chronos*, which means 'chronological time', linear time; the other is *Kairos*, which means 'time which is fulfilled, the right time'. The second definition is used in the story from Mark. The right moment in history has happened, the moment that is full of meaning, and Jesus is now here. Through all of history, creation has been waiting for the coming of the One who would fully show forth the things of God. That One is Jesus.

The Greek word for 'repentance', *Metanoia*, means 'a change in direction'; I was walking in one direction, and now I'm walking in another. Jesus is inviting us to turn around and follow him. When he says, 'Believe in the gospel of God', he means, 'put your trust in what I am about'. Believing means more than intellectual assent or emotional enthusiasm, it means 'to lean on'.

A missionary was trying to explain to a group of South Sea islanders what 'belief' meant. The island vocabulary had no word for it. Then the missionary saw an islander leaning against a tree with the full weight of his body. He asked the islander for the word for what he was doing and he used it to describe belief! Jesus is saying that he has come to show us this new life in himself; lean on it yourselves, put your life on this. Believe it and follow his example. Throughout his teaching we hear Jesus asking us to come and see what God's kingdom is like.

In the Gospel of John, chapter three, Jesus told Nicodemus that unless he was 'born from above' he would not be able to see the Kingdom. What Jesus meant was that unless God's Spirit works in our hearts we cannot begin to see how important his purposes are. When you ask people what it means to be a Christian, very often they will say 'living a good life,' or 'being nice to others,' or 'trying to be good.' That is not the definition of being a Christian. Christians are people who are about the Kingdom agenda of Jesus. Christians follow a different way of living that comes from a different way of seeing, 'seeing' God's agenda.

The kingdom agenda

One of the places where we can see something of that Kingdom agenda is in the Gospel of Matthew, chapters five to seven, in the Sermon on the Mount. It is a compilation of a lot of Jesus' teachings. Let's look at some of these teachings and see why it isn't easy to be a Christian!

Love your enemy

> You have heard that it was said, 'You shall love your
> neighbour and hate your enemy.' But I say to you, Love
> your enemies and pray for those who persecute you, so
> that you may be sons (and daughters) of your Father who
> is in heaven; for he makes his sun rise on the evil and on
> the good, and sends rain on the just and on the unjust.
> For if you love those who love you, what reward have you?
> Do not even the tax collectors do the same? And if you
> salute only your brethren, what more are you doing than
> others? Do not even the Gentiles do the same? You,
> therefore, must be perfect, as your heavenly Father is
> perfect (5:43–47).

Jesus asks us to love our enemies. 'Enemies' in this
passage are people who are single-mindedly out to
oppose who we are, to defame us, to tear us apart, to
speak evil of us, to work against us. When Jesus talks
about loving that kind of person, is it possible? Can we
bless those people and not speak evil of them, can we
not retaliate, can we offer them everything in our power
to make their lives worthwhile? This is the radical nature
of the Kingdom life. We must bless the person who is
tearing us apart.

Is this easy? Is this the simple Christian life that
everybody knows about? No, this is a radical life to
which Jesus is calling his followers. Even when someone
persecutes us, we are not to speak evil against them,
not even in subtle ways, but we are to see that their
lives are blessed.

When somebody claims they are a Christian because
they follow the Sermon on the Mount, I always ask if
they have read it recently. This is a sobering life we are
called to. What happens when somebody, out of their

own sense of being touched, healed and loved by God, does not feel a need to retaliate against persecution? When we have no need to be right, we can actually say to the offending party, 'God bless you,' and mean it. Have you ever seen the bumper sticker which says, 'Love your enemies, it'll drive them crazy!'? There's a lot of truth in that!

But what do we do if somebody continues to abuse us? We are not asked to be doormats. Loving our enemy is active not passive. Each situation demands an answer to the question, 'How can I love this enemy?' Look at Jesus who was unjustly arrested, unjustly charged, and sentenced to be crucified by government authorities who could not have cared less about him. Yet Jesus didn't strike back. He faced it all with tremendous spiritual strength and said nothing in his own defence. He loved his enemies and he died for them. Loving your enemies is a part of Kingdom life. Are you ready for that? That's what it means to be a Christian.

Treasures in heaven

> Do not lay up for yourselves treasures on earth, where moth and rust consume and where thieves break in and steal, but lay up for yourselves treasures in heaven, where neither moth nor rust consumes and where thieves do not break in and steal. For where your treasure is, there will your heart be also. (Matthew 6:19–21).

Jesus is saying that material things we have or desire can dominate our lives, but do not last.

A married couple in our church decided together that the wife would give up her job as a lawyer in order to have more time for their children. Right before this, they had made a decision to give five per cent of their income to the church, hoping in the future to raise it to ten per cent (a 'tithe'). But that decision had been based on two incomes. When one of them quit work they had to ask the question, 'Where is our treasure going to be?' They concluded that they had been basing their lives on what they wanted and not on what they needed and were going to have to give up certain things. There is a big difference between the two. They began to look more carefully at their business life. They began tithing. They looked at how they spent their time and changed it towards their family. They didn't find this easy to do, but as they reordered their lives they found some real freedom.

Jesus is telling us that where our security is, our hearts will be also. If we begin to 'lay up treasure in heaven', building up our own spiritual lives in God, then our priorities will change. For many of us, finance is where the rubber hits the road. Can we really trust God to provide what we need?

The poor and broken

> 'For I was hungry and you gave me food, I was thirsty and you gave me drink, I was a stranger and you welcomed me, I was naked and you clothed me, I was sick and you visited me, I was in prison and you came to me.' Then the righteous will answer him, 'Lord, when did we see thee hungry and feed thee, or thirsty and give thee drink? And when did we see thee a stranger and welcome thee, or naked and clothe thee? And when did we see thee sick or in prison and visit thee?' And the King will answer them, 'Truly, I say to you, as you did it to one of the least of these my brethren, you did it to me.' (Matthew 25:35–40).

Another part of the Kingdom agenda is God's care for the poor and broken of the world. God calls us to be the main instruments of his ministry to others in need. How often do we walk by a homeless person and wish 'he' would go away, or someone would do something about 'her'. The 'someone' is us. Today, as I write this, I am seeing the most wonderful assortment of people in my parish welcoming homeless people to 'rest awhile' in our church building. There is food available, there is a place to sit, there is companionship, there are people who are willing to help with references for housing and medical care. And, I suspect, before long there will be people who will start agitating with the city to provide better services for those in need! We are Christ's hands and feet and heart, we are the ones who see in the poor and broken in the world the ministry of Christ at work.

Living the kingdom life

As we look at the ministry of Jesus we are aware, not only of what he says, but what he does. He tells us that not only will we do the things he did, but greater ones still (John 14:12–14). What are the things which he does that he says we will do?

When God healed Harold (Chapter 1) of his heart problem through my prayer, he did it without my cooperation or understanding. Think what he can do with our active involvement!

In my last parish in New York we decided to take Jesus at his word and start praying for the sick. I know there are some big questions about why some people are healed and others are not, but we decided to pray for the sick anyway, because Jesus tells us to do it. If there is a chance that one person may be healed by our being faithful we must do so. For nearly all of the first two years that we prayed in this way, not only did people not get better, many became worse. In some cases the ones who were praying for the sick caught the same illnesses! That was discouraging! We had to coach and encourage each other to continue praying each Sunday. I have since often found this to be the case, that when this type of ministry starts up, not much seems to happen initially. But we kept at it.

One Sunday a couple came to church who had stopped by the previous day. The husband was an architect, and the wife was a lawyer. They were very sophisticated. They had been married for a while and had just had a baby, which they brought along with them, holding him in their arms. They were desperate. One chance in ten million had given the wife a virulent form of cancer associated with childbirth and she had developed brain cancer. Her hair had fallen out from the chemotherapy treatments. Finally, the doctors told her there was nothing more they could do. The couple had been walking past the church the previous day and stumbled in, feeling that God was their last chance. So our administrator told them to come back on Sunday.

Our prayer team had a batting average of zero. We were warned beforehand that these folks would be coming to church. At the end of the service when I invited the sick to come forward for prayer, these two came running. They knelt at the altar rail and said, 'Please help us.' It was very poignant, watching this mother holding onto her newborn baby, weeping and desperate for help. The people on our healing team were touched and looked at me as if to say 'What are we to do?' I told them to go for it! They began to pray and, as usual, nothing seemed to happen. So we decided to continue to pray for them.

Members of the parish prayed with this woman (and for her) every single day—day in and day out. When she was in the hospital, when she was throwing up, when the baby was screaming, when her husband was in despair, the prayer team stayed with them. It came to the point where we had a daily chart on our office door marking her progress. She would seem better one day and then become worse. Then, slowly a change took place.

A year later, when their son was a toddler, the woman stood in front of the congregation and held up a sheet of paper and read it to us. It was a report from her doctor which told her that she had no trace of cancer in her, and that he had no explanation for it. After she read it she picked up her son and said, 'I am well. I am thrilled to know that I no longer have any cancer in my body, but far more important than that is the fact that I have come to learn of the love of Christ through these praying people who were with me and my family every day. Even if I were going to die within a week that knowledge would be far more important than the healing I have had.' Shortly after that their son was baptized. They moved to Hawaii. Her healing was checked every six months for three years by doctors and they finally told her to stop coming back! When I last heard from them, they were all doing fine.

I believe that even though the chemotherapy was doing something, she was healed through prayer. And not just physically—her whole life was healed. That is the ministry Jesus gave us to carry on. We can't be perfunctory about it, we have to stay with it, it's the task we have been given. It is only when we are Kingdom-minded and trust that God is a loving God who will touch people's lives, that we can persevere although nothing appears to be happening.

Jesus still does the things he did when he walked the earth, but he does them through us. He moves through us, by his Spirit. I no longer worry so much about those who don't get well; I worry about those we don't pray for who might get well if we were faithfully praying. And you and I are the ones Jesus chose to carry on his work. We need to claim and expand God's love for the world through these kinds of ministries, not on television, but in a quiet and faithful, gracious and loving way, where we are.

Naturally supernatural

We all have blocks in our lives—we have disbelief and sin—and we need to get rid of these if we are to function properly. In order to be able to do what Jesus wants us to do, we need to be what I call 'naturally supernatural'. There is a film called *Viva Christo Rey*, which means 'Long Live Christ the King'. It's the story of a Jesuit priest who has a ministry among people who live in the garbage dumps of Juarez, Mexico. He teaches them how to pray for one another and how to support each other. He started working in the prisons in Juarez and across the border in El Paso, Texas, finding housing and jobs for released prisoners and their families. The movie shows what it means to be naturally supernatural.

The people have a farm where they grow food, but they don't often appear to have enough to go around. If they have food for a hundred people and four hundred show up to eat, the priest and the people just pray that, like the loaves and fishes (Mark 8:1–10), the food will multiply. He doesn't even say long prayers, he just says, 'Lord, feed them all.' And the food multiplies. Because of this, the people have come to expect miracles as part of their daily life. It is a powerful testimony to God's ability to work supernaturally in a natural situation.

Jesus is Lord

We must make Jesus Christ not only Saviour but also the Lord of our lives. Jesus has to call the shots. We are no longer in charge of our lives, he is. When first century Christians met each other in the street they would say 'Jesus is Lord!' It would be a proclamation of their own faith, but they would also say it to each other as an encouragement. They would also have symbols of fish on their houses, the Greek word for which, *Icthus*, spells out the initials of 'Jesus Christ, God's Son, Saviour'. These were people who believed that Jesus was in charge of their whole lives. That is what 'Jesus is Lord' means. We must desire more than anything to live for him and his Kingdom life.

We need to be able to take the final step and commit the whole of our lives to him. When we recognize we cannot live in our own strength Jesus will enable us to do so by empowering us with his Spirit. That is when the adventure of the Christian faith begins.

It might take us into places of conflict with the world, but when it does the world will see that following Jesus is more than just belief. One of the most powerful movies I have seen shows this well. It is a documentary called *Weapons of the Spirit*, about the people of the village of Le Chambon in France, a place formed by the Huguenot Protestant tradition. It is the true story about the Nazi occupation of France during the Second World War. The people of the village decided to protect and hide escaping Jews. The film is both humorous because of the ingenuity of the places used for the hiding, and very powerful in its depiction of how natural the people's faith was in response to the challenge of their daily life. Again and again, when the interviewer pressed the villagers for an explanation of why they did what they did, they seemed bewildered by all the fuss. 'It was what Jesus would have us do,' they said. What became clear was that this was indeed a natural outgrowth of the Lordship of Christ in their lives. When the challenge came, they rose to the occasion because it was how they lived already.

That is what happens when Jesus not only is glorified in a grand liturgy in Canterbury Cathedral, but also in Le Chambon, and Beverly Hills, and in all the corners of the earth. The life we are living is no longer our own, but his life in us.